THE
"OXFORD MOVEMENT:"

Strictures

ON THE

"PERSONAL REMINISCENCES,"
AND REVELATIONS

OF

DR. NEWMAN, MR. OAKELEY, AND OTHERS.

BY THE

REV. ROBERT MAGUIRE, M.A.

Clerical Secretary of the Islington Protestant Institute.

"BONA FIDES, REIPUBLICÆ TUTAMEN."

SECOND EDITION.

LONDON:

SEELEY, JACKSON, AND HALLIDAY, 54, FLEET STREET.
EDWARD FORD, ISLINGTON GREEN.

1855.

Price Fourpence.

Reprinted from the Church of England Quarterly Review.

Meaden, Printer High Street, Clapham.

THE
"OXFORD MOVEMENT."

THE " Oxford Movement," as it has been popularly designated, has for some years past, occupied much of public
attention. It has been felt that an under current has been
making its way beneath the very bed of the Isis, and has already
broken forth here and there, giving manifest indications of
its existence, disclosing its secret channels, and anon, by a
kind of sympathetic influence, commingling its waters with
the Tiber; into which, notwithstanding distance and inter-
vening seas, it flows by an easy confluence, without collision
and without spray, and thence holds on its joint current,
bearing onward to a boundless ocean of futurity many a
hapless bark destined to no certain end, save one of ruin
and of wreck, even the " shipwreck of *faith*."

We speak of the under current of Popish tendencies and
semi-Popish tenets which have more or less characterized
certain features of Oxford life and education during a quarter
of a century past; tenets and tendencies which have had but
one master object, one aim, one ultimate design, namely, the
infusion of a decided Papal element into the very nursery of
our Church, and the planting of Romish sympathies in one
of the most productive seed plots of our National Ecclesias-
tical Institution. Of these tendencies our venerable Primate,
when Bishop of Chester, gave a timely warning :—" It is
daily assuming," said his lordship, " a more serious and
alarming aspect, and threatens a revival of the worst evils of
the Romish system. Under the specious pretence of defer-
ence to antiquity, and respect for the primitive models, the
foundations of our Church are undermined by men who
dwell within her walls; and those who sit in the Reformers'
seat are traducing the Reformation."

The forewarning was not premature—the augury was
strictly true. Results have proved how set was the final
end, and how determinate was the wily counsel of those who
fostered and encouraged the movement; and who, under the

academic garb and invested with university authority, led on, to the brink of the precipice many for whose souls they must absolutely render an account at the bar of God, the Judge of all. Secrets there were in that design; cunning devices in the working out of the same; facts and principles were strangely distorted and twisted Romeward, and the most carefully guarded portions of our Protestant formularies were, by a most dishonourable process, perverted to a Romish use and tortured into a Romish sense.

Who then were the guiding stars of this erratic course? Whose were the minds that directed the " movement?" Who pulled the strings of this strangely diversified and intricate machinery? And who were the agents in conducting the deep laid scheme to its ultimate issue?

At first we laboured under manifest disadvantages. Suspicions, vague and unsatisfactory, alighted on certain heads; but, then, mere suspicions are not palatable to any and are very irksome to all. There are but few among us who would desire to cultivate a suspicious temper or a suspecting mind. Hence matters proceeded to their final and fatal consummation—no justice being rendered on the promoters and chief leaders of the plot. By and bye, however, one and another of these crossed the " Rubicon." Some of these were led to take this step of separation by reason of pressure from within—some to save appearances—some because their work was done, and they and their principles had become so transparent that none would henceforth trust them at *this* side of the stream. But all these when embosomed in Rome, were to us a happy riddance. They proved by a large induction, the real tendencies of the movement;—perversions acted as a warning and a timely notice to many who were already *en route*, and recalled them from their wanderings. While the *prestige* and influence of the respective positions of the perverts instantly and suddenly ceased.

Nor was this all. Still greater advantages accrued from the secessions; for from the other side and from the ground of their destination men, long time dishonest, have looked back and wondered at the still continued dishonesty of their former comrades; and those who themselves have been highly reprehensible, have ventured to chide the continued inconsistency of the men who first prompted *them* to the adoption of principles which naturally and inevitably led them to plunge into the deep dark gulf beneath. And in most cases, there have been " Confessions" made, and " Personal Reminiscences" vouchsafed, which open up many curious revelations and disclose many secret springs—all more or less descriptive of the *modus operandi*—all highly instructive and very deeply suggestive. From these and such as these we have learned more since their perversion than we could have possibly gathered from the secret plans and under-current of their antecedent conduct. In fact, when they had accomplished their design, as far as they could accomplish it, and had escaped from the jurisdiction of law and justice, they then reveal their dishonest deeds, and disclose their secret mines and hidden works of darkness. Too late for the victims of the past; but just in time to save many from a similar course of action, and from a like destruction.

For example, Dr. Newman has made some startling disclosures relative to his own conduct in this respect, while holding and exercising his office in the University. Dr. Newman is inseparably associated with the series of publications called " *The Tracts for the Times,*" which periodically issued from the press, and continued for some considerable time, and far longer than they ought, to imbue the minds of the students of our Universities and the public generally with Popish sentiments and sympathies. These works were written, to a great degree, in a novel and attractive style, with a faint semblance of Protestantism, but with a thoroughly Popish tendency. Their great object was to modify and palliate the worst errors of Rome, by glossing over their worst features and concealing their deleterious character ; in fact fact an effort was made, by the infusion of such infinitesimal doses of diluted Popery, to administer the deadly draught to its very dregs—to poison the very heart of our Protestantism, the very seats of learning ;—and in an evil hour, and by the strategy of one or more within the camp, to open the gates of our city and remove our bulwarks, and thus admit the stalking horse of seeming Protestantism, but in reality a ponderous engine pregnant and teeming with Popish agencies, within the sacred walls of our Sion. These measures were all the more successful, when practised on a people which had well nigh forgotten what Popery really is, both in spirit and in practice. England had dwelt securely, too much so. Our people were " at ease in Sion." They anticipated no aggression, no invasion of their dearest birthright; still less did they expect or prepare for a side attack, conducted as it was, and faithlessly perpetrated within our own camp, by those who wore our livery, were in our pay, and *professed* our doctrines.

Of some of the most insidious and therefore dangerous of these " Tracts for the Times," Dr. Newman has avowed himself the author. In these there occurred incidentally certain strong epithets *against* the Church of Rome; but in this consisted the chief danger. For, while intended to accomplish, and in reality accomplishing, the work of Rome, these pamphlets were so cautiously and disingenuously interspersed with anti-Popish expressions, as to disarm suspicion, and render the poison all the more palatable by reason of a slender Protestant element slightly introduced. This was the then latent and now obvious design; and this design, to a great extent, has been achieved.

In this Dr. Newman shall be his own witness; he will speak for himself and tell his own tale. In his Preface to his *Essay on Developement*, written in 1845, he unveils the "Tractarian" mystery, and at the same time reveals the dishonesty which secretly lurked behind this fair seeming movement. In that Preface Dr. Newman thus wrote:—"In 1834 I also used of certain doctrines of the Church of Rome the epithets, 'unscriptural,' 'profane,' 'impious,' 'bold,' 'unwarranted,' 'blasphemous,' 'gross,' 'monstrous,' 'cruel,' 'administering deceitful comfort,' and 'unauthorised,' in Tract 38."

All these epithets Dr. Newman *retracts;* and proceeds further to say:—"Perhaps I have made other statements in a similar tone, and that, again, when the statements themselves were unexceptionable and true."

Now, when we come to inquire into Dr. Newman's motives for thus expressing himself with reference to the Church of Rome—when we examine why and wherefore he did thus write *against* that very system which at that very time he cherished, we discover the answer in the following paragraph, quoted in continuation of the above:—

"If you ask me," writes Dr. Newman, "how an individual could venture, not simply to hold, but to publish, such views of a communion so ancient, so wide spreading, so fruitful in saints; I answer, that *I said to myself* 'I am not speaking *my own* words, I am but following almost a *consensus* of the divines of my Church. *They* have even used the strongest language against Rome, even the most able and learned of them. I wish to throw myself into *their* system. While I say what *they* say, *I am safe.* Such views, too, are *necessary for our position.*' Yet I have reason to fear still, that such language is to be ascribed, in no small measure, to an impetuous temper, a hope of *approving myself* to persons I respect, and a wish *to repel the charge of Romanism !*"

Ah! Dr. Newman! *Habemus confitentem reum.* The culprit stands self-accused. You now avow that for so many years you thus trifled with your own conscience; and in order to impose upon the too confiding youth that were entrusted to your care, and to gain the too credulous and unsuspecting public that lent an ear to your wiles, you seasoned the dishonest writings of modern Tractarians with a sprinkling of the salt of the Church—the honest, heartfelt, and outspoken declarations of our ancient divines! "You said *to yourself!*" But why did you not say to others what you whispered to yourself in the privacy of your own bosom? What could the public know of your silent musings for so many years? You expected they would give the credit of your Protestantism, such as it was, to Tillotson and Tenison, Whitby and Stillingfleet, in hope that they would, *pari passu*, imbibe all the Popery of the Tracts, as though from the same sound Protestant authorities. You thought to adapt your teaching to the taste of the unsuspecting, by gilding its nauseous and offensive qualities. The gilding was borrowed, the drug was your own. And while you thus wore the mask and appeared in public in a garb, (not your own, but) assumed for a purpose, you say, "you were safe!" Yes! for while you would be read and followed as Dr. Newman, you would, occasionally, and at proper intervals, be mistaken for a Jewell or a Chillingworth. And this disingenuous conduct you allege as even "necessary to your position;" and all with the main object of having yourself "approved" by friends, and in order "to repel the charge of Romanism!"

This is a species of honesty which even the morality of this wicked world would abhor. Mammon itself would scorn to countenance such a mode of conducting business. Such principles would in a trice be scouted from the Exchange and the banking house by the mercantile world and by business men. But in Rome it is all consistent, quite correct, indigenous. Hence in the "bosom" of the Church of Rome this man finds a welcome; he enters, and there he finds himself quite "at home." "The end sanctifies the means;" and if the end be vile, what matter what kind of road conducts thereto.

This *résumé* of Dr. Newman's career, though perhaps by this time an old story and oft told, we introduce as a fitting prelude to more recent revelations, and as an illustration of a movement the sum total of whose secrets we have never, and very probably shall never, be fully informed of. "Confessions" are still from time to time delivered, containing fresh evidence of the duration, the depth. and the inveteracy of the "Oxford Movement" towards Rome.

The Rev. F. Oakeley has just issued to the public some " Personal Reminiscences"* of his Oxford life and some disclosures as to the Tractarian doings in that University. He, in fact, turns king's evidence, and as such exhibits himself, if possible, in a more dishonourable light than even his most devoted fellow-labourers; and invests himself with a most unenviable notoriety in connexion with the unworthy history of this movement. And, curious enough, he disclaims by anticipation the charge of "*egotism!*" If this be "egotism," we may hope that ere long that gentle weakness shall be quite eradicated from the human breast. But such an introductory disclaimer is not altogether without a parallel.

"Confessions" and "autobiographies" are just now very popular. The autobiography of a celebrated American has gained a thousandfold circulation, simply by reason of the enormity of the antecedents and the cool self-possession—the *nonchalance* of the narrator. Some men glory in their shame, and quail not before the public indignation that must naturally arise in hearing of past deeds of cunning and mischief. Such confessions may tend to amuse by the mere enterprise and adventure which characterise them: how cunning outwitted honesty, and deep laid schemes suddenly surprised the unsuspecting. There is also much romance of real life to be anticipated from one who has been " behind the scenes." He can tell how phantoms have been put forward and have impressed the byestanders with the idea of actual reality—how disguises have been admirably adapted, and have positively beguiled one's better judgment—how the eye has been deceived by art, the ear by sound, all the senses by artifice and fraud. And, worse than all, one must be prepared to hear from the chief actor in the scene the chuckle of conscious triumph, which ere long greets the ear of the dupe, who has been victimised by the imposition.

The " Confessions" of Mr. Oakeley partake somewhat of these features. Having for about twenty years transacted his part in the " Oxford Movement," he now steps forward as the " retired manager" to reveal what he has been doing all the time, and *how* he succeeded in his attempt. He gathers together those who confess to him, and in turn makes *his* confession to them. Rather the public is his priest, to the public he confesses, though not in the spirit of penitence, but with the bravado of one rejoicing in his offence. Will

---

* " Personal Reminiscences of the ' Oxford Movement;' &c., addressed to the Islington (Rom.) Catholic Popular Club."

the public absolve him?   And after all, Mr. Oakeley might well adopt the prefatory observation of the American auto-biography—"though a portion of my 'confessions' may by some be considered *injudicious*, I prefer frankly to 'acknowledge the corn,' wherever I have had a hand in plucking it."

Too long and too confidingly, indeed, did the Church of England entrust a portion of her precious " cornfield" to the hands of one who faithlessly discharged the sacred duty and betrayed the sacred trust confided to his care.   But *we* shall not bear witness: he shall bear witness to himself.   Mr. Oakeley proceeds to trace his " earliest personal reminiscences," which, be it remembered, are coeval with the first beginning of the Movement :—

" My earliest 'personal reminiscences' of an inroad upon the old fashioned religionism of Oxford, date from the Regius Professor-ship of Dr. Charles Lloyd, the tutor of the late Sir Robert Peel, who received from that minister, about the year 1827, the appoint-ment to the Bishoprick of Oxford.   Dr. Lloyd was a clergyman of great attainments and unusual ability. . . . . . By early education and academical connexion, Dr. Lloyd was of course a staunch Pro-testant; but on succeeding to the responsible office of Divinity Professor, and finding himself possessed of the influence which his learning and ability, joined to a remarkable facility of gaining upon the affections of his pupils, gave him over the young men of his class, he contrived to extricate himself more or less from the tram-mels of his position, and to run out, in what Oxford men would call, a 'new line.'   He accordingly selected as the subject of a course of divinity lectures, the History and Structure of the Anglican Prayer-book,—a subject which led him, and with him his pupils, to the examination of the Missal and Breviary, as the source from which the principal contents of the Prayer-book had been taken."

" Behold how great a matter a little fire kindleth !"   Who could ever have dreamt that such allusions to the constitu-tion of the Prayer-book should have produced such a " Movement ?"   It is probable the Divinity Professor was just as right in his premises, as it is certain some of his pupils were wrong in their conclusions.   That the Roman Missal and the English Prayer-book contain *some* prayers in common is quite true ;   and to our mind unobjectionable, provided those prayers be such as are addressed to God only through the intercession of the Son, as all those held in common *are* addressed.   But that " the *principal contents* of the Prayer-book" have been taken from the Roman Missal and Breviary we wholly deny.   Of the Breviary we retain little or nothing —if we except the Psalms of David, of which we hope our Romish friends do not claim to be the donors.   From the

Missal we have preserved some ancient and orthodox prayers, in fact, all that was found in it in the shape of wheat, as contradistinguished to the chaff. Nor are even these the peculiar and inalienable property of Rome; she, too, has receved them from others, and from many sources accumulated her body of Prayer. The epistles and gospels we, of course, derive from the Bible, not from the Missal. And such passages as we have derived therefrom, our Church rendered into the English form, so that they are "understanded of the people;" unlike to the Church of Rome, which conveys them in the (to the public) unintelligible channel of the Latin tongue.

In this the Reformers exercised a wise discretion. Their duty was not to pull down this or that because it was *Christian*, but because it was *Popish*. Hence they conserved the parts unsullied by error, and cast the bad away. They found in the Missal and as the staple constitution of the Breviary, much that was false, legendary, superstitious, and directly unscriptural; these portions were of modern date, and had from time to time been introduced in order to countenance and encourage the growing superstitions and errors of the Roman Catholic Church; as, for example, the invocation of Saints, worship of the Host and of the Cross, and such like. All these were expunged; and the portions which agreed with Holy Writ (these were the most ancient too,) were duly set apart, "taken out," as an old writer says, "as gold from dross, as the precious from the vile."

So much for the Missal and the Breviary. But how could the Regius Professor's prelections have tended thus to originate such a Movement as that which Mr. Oakeley now reviews? It appears that this intelligence thus conveyed by Dr. Lloyd was quite a new idea to Oxford and Oxford men, and in a moment the whole class became prepossessed in favour of the Ritual books of Rome. A sudden demand was made on the stock of a Roman Catholic bookseller; and the Missals and Breviaries lying in store in the warehouses in New Bond Street were speedily under commission to Oxford; and like the dragon teeth which Cadmus sowed, were quickly to become the seed of a new generation—of Churchmen, who were with Missal and Breviary to proceed *en route* to Rome. Mr. Oakeley proceeds to observe:—" On a sudden, and without any explained cause, Mr. Booker's repository in New Bond Street, was taxed even to the full extent of its ample resources, to furnish liturgies and office-books, for the Oxford students."

But here there occurred an obstacle. "Mr. Booker," continues Mr. Oakeley, "was too good a (Roman) Catholic to treat such a demand as a mere matter of business, and, as he dared not hope for a miracle, shrewdly suspected a plot." So that, it appears, Mr. Booker was not quite sure how to act, and had his own misgivings, and needed some mutual acquaintance to instruct and reassure him.

This mutual acquaintance was at once forthcoming. That friend of Missals and Breviaries, *anterior to* 1827, was Mr. Oakeley himself! He thus narrates the circumstances :— " By a singular coincidence it happened that the only Protestant in Oxford whom Mr. Booker knew was myself, and that the only (Roman) Catholic in the world whom I knew was Mr. Booker; and I believe *I* was the means of allaying his apprehensions, *and securing a free importation of Missals and Breviaries into Oxford !!* "

This is much like the language of contrabandists and savours much of illicit and dishonourable traffic with Babylon. All this was prior to the year 1827, since which date a whole generation has grown to manhood, and even then, at so remote a period, was Mr. Oakeley found befriending Rome, and doing the part of the traitor before he finally issued forth as a deserter. Truly his experience has been of long standing, his hand early tried in Rome's service, and his final *exit* from among us too long delayed for one so very precocious in his Popish attainments as an undergraduate. Had he even then gone up " for honours" to *Rome*, we fancy he would have merited investment as a Knight of the Roman Missal and Breviary !

One cannot imagine why an occasional orthodox prayer from the Roman Missal should have created such a *furore* in Oxford and such a demand on poor Mr. Booker: as well should the Roman Catholic people make a sudden demand for the Koran of Mahomet, because it contains some allusion to their new dogma of the Immaculate Conception—as well might they buy up large stores of Buddist Rituals, and Hindoo idols, because the Roman Ritual strongly resembles the one, and the images of Rome are characteristically like to those of heathen countries ! We may, perhaps, by parity of reason, shortly expect an unparalleled demand for Protestant Bibles, inasmuch as the Romish translations have gradually been approximating to our version as a standard of accurate rendering ; or, very probably, a large demand for Greek Rituals from our friends in St. Petersburg, because we have presumed to select some ancient and orthodox prayers from the old Greek Liturgies also !

How it came to pass then that such fruits have resulted, ostensibly at least, from Dr. Lloyd's Divinity Lectures, will appear plainly and palpably from Mr. Oakeley's notice of certain names that gathered to these lectures—names, some of which we recognize as no unknown ones in this Movement. "To the lectures of Dr. Lloyd," writes Mr. Oakeley, "resorted John Henry Newman, and Edward Pusey, (though of older standing than the majority of the class); and among those somewhat junior, Mr. (late Archdeacon) Wilberforce, Mr. Froude, the late Bishop of Salisbury, and many others, including myself."

Whence came these older heads, as out of due time, mingling with junior classes? What evil was there premeditated; what "Movement" inaugurated? With such names as those of Newman, and Pusey, and (unhappily) Wilberforce, and others, we can expect—(we are not now reasoning *a priori*, results render that quite superfluous)—we can expect nothing good, nothing conducive to the good of the Church of England. Most of these have since transferred their allegiance from England to Rome—were then "*almost*," but now are "*altogether*" Romanists. And we must still deplore and protest against the continuance among us, in our colleges, our pulpits, and our schools, of many persons whose hearts are, we fear, wholly given to Rome, while they still retain the outward garb and guise of Protestantism. Some of these have grown old in the service, and their grey hairs must oft remind them how long they have lived but to promote a system, in all its parts antagonistic to that which they *profess* to follow. The pupils have passed over, while some of the masters still remain among us. In fact, the Romanizing party have led more to Romanism in this country than has Rome herself.

Bishop Lloyd's death caused a temporary cessation and disuse of Missals and Breviaries in Oxford. Mr Oakeley says that the bishop died a victim to the cause of "Catholic Emancipation." "He talked himself in the House of Lords into a fever, of which in three weeks he died." Not so sudden or inglorious a death, however, as that of Pope Clement VII., who, when he was requested to resign the Pontificate to the rival anti-Pope, Boniface IX, "conceived so great grief that he fell sick, and died of apoplexy on the 16th September, in the year 1394."* Nor yet in so unchristian a manner as that same Boniface IX., who when he

* Dupin, vol. ii. 511. Ed. 1723. Dub.

entered on "Billingsgate" with his rival, Benedict XIII., and was by him called a Simonist, &c., "was enraged to that degree, that he fell sick and died in three days after!"* Nor yet so basely as Pope Alexander VI., who, according to the Roman Catholic historian of the Sorbonne, "died on the 18th August, in the year 1503, having taken by a mistake that *poison* which *he* had prepared for poisoning the cardinals whom he had invited!" †

The lull was but temporary. How could the Movement sleep while such men directed its progress. The ball once set in motion, and receiving fresh impulse from time to time, must, if not checked by a speedy and powerful hand, increase in its velocity, and still continue to move until it reaches its destination. The charger, eager for the race, and reined in by a rider determined *per fas ac nefas* to finish his course, will not stop short of the goal. In this race Romeward, a Newman, a Pusey, a Wilberforce, a Froude, and such like, entered the lists—themselves to run the race, and to train others for the same course in time to come, (Mr. Oakeley "securing a free importation" of materials!)

Mr. Froude gained considerably a-head at first. "In him," says Mr. Oakeley, "Dr. Lloyd's teaching on the subject of liturgies found a mind ripe at the age of one and twenty, for receiving impressions favourable even to the *Roman Church, and strongly adverse to the Reformation.*"

The next act in this Movement was the publication of the Oxford " *Tracts for the Times.*" And here Mr. Oakeley commits himself to a most unfortunate illustration, but *so* true and *so* telling that it really does one's heart good to hear him thus describe it. He observes:—" But the lesson was but slowly and reluctantly learned by the great body of the University, that the *wooden horse* which stalked so heavily and so majestically along, was full of warriors, armed *cap-à-piè,* for an encounter. At length came forth the celebrated Tract XC. &c."

Can it be that Mr. Oakeley, in his zeal for the Oxford Movement, or perhaps in the overcrowded state of his memory with the sudden flow of " Personal Reminiscences," has forgotten the true story of Virgil's " wooden horse?" To refresh his reminiscences in this respect, we would remind him, and at all events inform his " Popular Club," that there was once a siege of a celebrated city, Troy, (of which, by the way, Dr. Morris, of Southwark, is the present Roman

---

* Dupin, vol. ii. p. 514.   † Ibid. vol. iii. p. 44.

Catholic bishop!) The Greeks were baffled in their attempts to take this stronghold; and like the allied armies "before Sebastopol" they desired to enter the city. After many obstinate encounters and alternating successes and defeats, they were still outside the walls of Troy. At length a crafty Greek, by name Sinon, contrived a "Movement," which would be likely to tell upon the strong old bulwarks that had held out a ten years' siege. A "wooden horse" was constructed, and soon its womb was filled with "warriors, armed *cap-à-piè*, for an encounter." But the difficulty was how to get it into the city. The crafty Sinon undertook this service, and accordingly obtained admission to the beleaguered city. Sinon was, in fact, "the only Greek in the world that was known" within its precincts. He professed himself a friend, and asked protection, and received it, and was trusted. He reported that the Greeks had fled, had raised the seige, and had left this huge horse as a trophy of their failure. The Trojans accordingly sallied out with unsuspecting zeal, danced around the monstrous horse, admired its grand proportions, and sung their songs of peace before it; and ultimately "the wooden horse stalked heavily and majestically along," passed the gates, and rested in the quadrangle of the city. The simple Trojans, a match for any Greeks in open warfare, were now duped; and then silently, and by stealth, at dead of night, the perjured Sinon approached the horse, opened its bars, unlocked its huge sides, and the "warriors, armed *cap-à-piè*" emerged from its dark inclosure and made short work of the city;— the ten years' seige was ended, and the sturdy battlements of Troy destroyed by the perfidy of *one man!*

This is the story of the "wooden horse"—that wooden horse is the "Oxford Movement," Mr. Oakeley himself being judge. It is pregnant with Rome's secret warriors, who lurk in its deep recesses—this is "necessary to their position;" and while they are there "they are safe!" And where and who is Sinon? There are many such; their name is Legion. But if there be one pre-eminently so, and *par excellence* entitled to the equivocal honour, it must be that man who, at the earliest outset, held conclave with the enemy, and who, according to his own confession, "was the means of securing *a free importation* of Missals and Breviaries into Oxford!" This is the modern Sinon—this the story of the modern "wooden horse," so unfortunately applied by Mr. Oakeley himself as an illustration of the "Oxford Movement."

But Mr. Oakeley proceeds, in continuation of the last quoted extract:—

" At length came forth the celebrated Tract XC., which effectually sounded the alarm, by propounding an interpretation of the Thirty-nine Articles, which would allow of the conscientious subscription of persons far gone in the road of Catholicism. . . The obnoxious tract had a mark set upon it by the ' Hebdomadal Board,' which served rather as an ' imprimatur ' than a stigma; and the enormous produce of its sale enabled its author to lay up materials of fresh *mischief* in the form of an excellent theological library. Meanwhile the argument of the tract was defended, and its theory of subscription, it must be confessed, improved upon. *All ' Roman doctrine' was let in* (and I am sure with the greatest *honesty* of purpose,) by the door which had been opened to admit merely the highest Anglicanism, &c."

Here lies the grand secret of the whole conspiracy. It was felt all along that the Thirty-nine Articles were too essentially Protestant to admit of any Popish tendencies in the Church of England. The Articles of the Church of England are distinctly defined, are purely scriptural, are wholly *anti-*Romish,—charged to the full with explicit Protestantism. As such the Thirty-nine Articles are and can be in no respect consistent with the Romeward tendencies of the Romanizers, Dr. Newman and his *confreres* felt this. Hence their evident difficulty. To *subscribe* these Articles was necessary to their tenure of office, benefice, or dignity; but to *believe* these Articles was inconsistent with their avowed principles. To solve this problem, which they found so difficult of solution, was the great *desideratum* of the " Oxford Movement." Hence the appearance of Tract No. XC., was hailed with acclamation. It elicited an unprincipled principle, " which," to use Mr. Oakeley's definition, " would allow of the *conscientious* subscription of persons *far gone* in the road of Catholicism."* In fact, it recommended a mode of subscription secretly qualified by mental reservation ; and these men, accordingly, have avowed that they subscribed the Articles,

---

* A recent pervert to the Church of Rome, Rev. W. H. Anderdon, Leicester, has lately revealed to an audience in the North of England, the steps of his progress to Rome. He began " with a notice of the causes which first tended to lead him away to Roman Catholicism, and prominent among these were the influences of his college life at Oxford, and an earnest study of the ' Tracts for the Times.' . . . *For many years* after he was *ordained* to the charge of a parish, he made a practice of regularly going *to confession*, but he did not deem it necessary to state the name of the clergyman to whom he confessed—suffice it to say, he was now an eminent priest in the [Roman] Catholic Church!"—*Sunderland Times*, quoted in *Tablet*, June 9th, 1855.

not in an honest, explicit, and unequivocal sense, but in a *non-natural* sense. What this crooked, *unnatural*, and equivocal mode may be, it would be difficult for any honest mind to understand. The invention of this very questionable theory is of itself sufficient to prove that the Church of England is essentially Protestant in her constitution and doctrine. And this very unmistakeable character of her Articles it is that attaches to her the large, and we trust increasing, body of her faithful children, who desire to maintain inviolate her original integrity, and to protect her old-fashioned realities from the innovations of these latter days. So long as the Church of England continues to hold her apostolic doctrine and rightful discipline, and retains the spirit which once reformed her after centuries of error, so long shall she ensure and command the willing respect and dutiful service of her people, and unite in a sure bond of peace and love the children whom God has given her.

There is perhaps no document, no embodiment of Christian doctrine, that has been so diversely handled, or so dishonourably dealt with, as the Thirty-nine Articles of the Church of England. In 1837 Dr. Newman designated the Articles as " a test *against Romanism;*"* and yet, soon after published the theory of Tract XC, whereby subscription might very consistently " let in all Roman doctrine."† At one time they are spoken of as " allowing of the conscientious subscription of persons far gone in the road of [Roman] Catholicism ;"‡ and when these parties find the staunch Protestantism of the Articles to resist the elastic pressure of such " conscientious" minds, they resort to abuse, and say, " The Thirty-nine Articles are *vile.*"§ And within the past few weeks further evidences have appeared of this uncandid characteristic of the Oxford Movement. In a brief memoir of the Rev. W. Palmer's recent secession to Rome, from the *Univers,*‖ we are informed that that gentleman had, on one occasion, actually foresworn all the Articles, in order to bring them into perfect unison with the Russo-Greek Church! He travelled into Russia, with a view to bringing about a union of the Church of England with the Greek Church! " He carried his request before the Synod of St. Petersburgh," says the memoir, " and assured them that, by the interpreta-

---

* Lect. on the Proph. Office, p. 287.   † Mr. Oakeley's Lect. p. 8.
‡ Mr. Oakeley's Lect. p. 4.   § *Rambler*, April, 1855, p. 261.
‖ *Tablet*, May 26th, 1855.

tion of the Thirty-nine Articles, given in *No. XC. of the* '*Tracts for the Times*,' those Articles were *capable* of explanation in a sense that relieved them from the imputation of heresy." The memoir accordingly proceeds :—

" The Russian Synod, not a little embarrassed by this novel claim on its functions, then deputed a theologian to examine the ' Thirty-nine Articles,' which compose the Anglican confession of faith. The result of this examination was, that the said Articles were discovered to contain no less than *forty-two heretical propositions ;* and Mr. Palmer was required solemnly to anathematize these before he could be admitted to Holy Communion in the ' Orthodox Russian Church.' The member of Oxford University went before the Synod, and *boldly pronounced the anathema against those of the propositions submitted to him*, which were propositions equally opposed to the doctrines of the [Roman] Catholic as of the Greek Russian Church, one of those doctrines being that of Transubstantiation."

Even in St. Petersburgh, with all their failings, they had not proceeded as far in Jesuitism and casuistry as the members of the " Oxford Movement." We only wonder these men never attempted to bring the Thirty-nine Articles into correspondence with the tenets of Mohammet or the Book of Mormon. One would be just as reasonable as the other, and all equally consistent with the " *non-natural* sense," which, after all, means *non-sense*. The Thirty-nine Articles are distinct to a tittle ; nice, even to a point ; Catholic, in the possession and defence of all Christian truth ; Protestant, in unmistakeable opposition to all Anti-Christian error. Such is the real character of the Thirty-nine Articles.

By such evasions and perversions of the radical characteristic of our Church, however, was " all Roman doctrine let in." Nothing more true ; and even though the sale of Tract XC. tended to replenish Dr. Newman's book-shelves, by reason of the condemnation affixed by the university ; yet we rejoice that the Tract is condemned. Strange, indeed, if it were otherwise. Its theory has no place amongst us ; " we have no such custom, neither the churches of God." Mr. Oakeley does well to occupy the breach on behalf of his friend of " thirty years' acquaintance," and to claim for him the character of honesty. Even Mr. Oakeley can see how natural such a charge of " insidiousness" must be. But before we receive Mr. Oakeley's testimony to Dr. Newman's probity, we ought to be assured of Mr. Oakeley's own position in this respect.

And here we may very fairly and opportunely quote the circumstances connected with Mr. Oakeley's secession from the Church of England. He continued his ostensible connexion with us—while holding all Romish doctrine—until the lay-ecclesiastical judge decided against him, and in the following words reproved his insincerity :—

"His (Mr. Oakeley's) own statement," remarked Sir Herbert Jenner Fust, " as to the conduct which he pursues when he is consulted upon the propriety of a person leaving the Church of England for the Church of Rome is, in fact, *an evasion.* His conduct, in outwardly professing to be a member of one church, whilst he is inwardly attached to the doctrines of another; and his declaration that he signs the Thirty-nine Articles, in a sense different from their grammatical construction, in which he knows they ought to be signed,—can hardly be reconciled with *integrity.*"

And again, the learned judge remarked :—

"I have already stated, that where the Articles are plain, distinct and definite, affording no room for doubt as to their real meaning, no attempt can be sanctioned which goes to distort their language, and so to extort by unfair means, if fair means will not do, a sense consistent with that ultra Catholic or Roman doctrine which Mr. Oakeley professes."*

This is a summary of Mr. Oakeley's own conduct for many a long year within the pale of our Church. And this leads us in the sequence of his Lecture, to other scenes and other phases of the Oxford Movement.

The scene is now shifted from the precincts of Oxford, and we are transferred to another locality. Mr. Oakeley proceeds thus :—"While Oxford was carrying on its work in its own way, a collateral and yet independent effort in the same direction was being made in a little chapel, 'not a hundred miles' from Cavendish Square." He means Margaret Chapel, of which he himself was sometime incumbent, and from which we may accordingly anticipate some additional revelations. Margaret Chapel is described by its former incumbent in no very flattering terms. Its name and its origin, its old clerk and his " brown wig," its huge pulpit and reading-desk; all were offensive to the eye of the man who, years before, had been the means of " securing a free importation of Missals and Breviaries into Oxford!" Mr. Oakeley states that, under its old *regime,* it passed into a fashionable chapel. It then fell into a kind of " modified Tractarianism." Its alternating changes and subsequent fate are thus briefly told :—" Under the last of these administrations (modified Tractarianism), it was almost deserted ; and as the bishop found it hopeless to fill the place of the outgoing minister, he accepted, not I

---

* Case of Hodgson *v.* Rev. F. Oakeley, by Dr. Bayford, pp. 134, 156.

believe without some misgivings, an offer from Oxford to undertake it."

The "Oxford Movement" henceforth enjoys the possession of a town house, and in the West End too. To this town residence were moved up certain indispensable materials for making this West End experiment successful, and worthy of its promoters ; that is to say, among the rest, a clergyman was appointed to the charge, schooled after the Tractarian model, and possessed of a "firm resolution to stand or fall by the religious principles he had learned." Accordingly, more attention was devoted to the shape and position of the pulpit, than to the orthodoxy of the preacher. The pulpit was "moved from its former position." " *Cœlum non animum mutant:*" they change their position, not their *dis*position, in Margaret Chapel. " The communion-table, now dignified with the name of an altar, exhibited its crimson frontal, its cross, and its candlesticks, whose unlighted candles were standing memorials of episcopal inflexibility, and emblems of patient hope. Not indeed that they were *always* unlighted ; for there came periodically the succession of night to day, and at times the elements favoured us with *a propitious fog !*"

See how the "Oxford Movement" delights in darkness, and comes from the land of fogs! The sunbeam is too bright for their doings ; the greater light that rules the day sheds too great a lustre on their deeds ; they must have candles also, to hide its brilliancy ; and would evidently prefer darkness, with dim candle-light, to noonday and the sunshine without candles. *Chacun à son gôut.* But such were the tendencies and predilections in Margaret Chapel under Mr. Oakeley's ministry.

And he has had his reward. " Margaret Chapel," continues Mr. Oakeley, " has yielded some scores of converts to the [Roman] Catholic Church, including *four* of its successive ministers ; and this, although it never aimed at anything but to promote the cause of the Church of England. It continued to do its work long after I quitted it, and has now merged into one of the most magnificent churches in England, which I have no doubt *will do its work also !*"

There is a contradiction somewhere here. Margaret Chapel " never aimed at anything but to promote the cause of the Church of England ;" and yet it was all the time " doing *its work*," and " will do *its work !*" " Its work," in one line, is to " promote the cause of the Church of England ;" and yet, in the next line, " its work" is to contribute " scores of converts to the Church of Rome !" Yes! to " promote the cause of the Church of England" was the pretence—to supply " scores to Rome" was the reality. Mr. Oakeley would doubtless have us to believe, that when he " outwardly professed to be a member of one church, while he was inwardly attached to the doctrines of another," he was " promoting the cause of the Church of England !" We could expect no other or more natural result from the course of conduct pursued in Margaret Chapel. Mr. Oakeley admits, that he and his colleagues voted the Church of England sufficiently broad, and latitudinarian enough to admit all Romish doctrine. Hence they continued their deadly work, and are now bold to say, what we hope will reach the ears of the bishops of the Church. "The bishops," he says, " will not move until they are compelled; and will find in the maturity of the work they have to overthrow, the penalty of their own procrastination !" And, true enough, had this disease been dealt with in time, or even now, with a powerful, prayerful hand, nerved by a sense of conscious duty and bounden right, the issue would be neither doubtful nor long deferred. Let the disease be tolerated, not to say fostered and encouraged, and these men will live on the procrastination and smile at the procrastinators, and then turn round to-morrow and reproach the weakness that bore with their un-Protestant, unscrupulous proceedings. We cannot but feel jealous that any one of these men should have it in his power thus to chide those in authority, who certainly have the means made ready to their hand, if they had but the will or the courage to use them to the furtherance of God's truth.

One more fact connected with the " Oxford Movement," to which our attention is directed by Mr. Oakley's lecture, is perhaps the most instructive, albeit of all the most eminently absurd. " I must let you into a secret," says Mr. Oakeley. "You must understand, then, that the idea of conversion to the [Roman] Catholic Church, which many persons at that time encouraged, was that, not of submission, one by one, to her authority, but of a *union* between the [Roman] Catholic Church and the Establishment;—or what were then called, the ' Churches of England and Rome.'" Could any scheme be more eminently preposterous ? that these few men should thus at this time of day dictate to the Church of England to unite with her most virulent enemy;—that we should thus retrace our steps, and find ourselves at the same point from which we were in God's mercy delivered at the time of the Reformation;—that we should thus vote the blood of the martyrs to have been vainly shed, and the great religious revolution of the sixteenth century to have been an idle and capricious change. Who were these men thus to assume, gratuitously, the office of spokesmen for the Church of England? " We, the British Nation," the well known preface to the lucubrations of the three tailors of Tooley Street, was not more presumptuous than this assumption on the part of the promoters of the Oxford Movement; thus providing for us the terms of capitulation before they themselves deserted to the enemy.

Yet such a Utopian scheme, such visionary speculations were seriously entertained, and even by Roman Catholics. " England was pictured to the fancy, as a willing and a flourishing dependency of the Church." Our cathedrals were instantly voted " natural homes" of Popish worship; and but for the limits to priestly power, would have been at once transubstantiated into Popish mass-houses. "Ruined abbeys" were in the twinkling of an eye themselves again. Papal imagination floated even over Lambeth, unscared by the deep shades of the dark Lollards' Tower and its " reminiscences," and seemed to ponder " what might not be the moral effect of a legantine commission, even on the Archbishop of Canterbury himself!"

These illusive dreams were interrupted by one grand obstacle. If the clergy of England were by fusion with Rome to become Popish priests, what was to be done with their *wives!* " If the natural good feeling of these ladies" writes the celibate, " did not lead them to desire a separate maintenance, the obstacle might be overcome by a temporary suspension of the law of clerical celibacy:"—he might have added, *convents* could be provided for " these ladies" where any and every Romish priest would be allowed freer access to them than their own husbands! This is what they have done with the wife of the Rev. Pierce Connolly, and what they still persist in doing. But why should wives, lawful wives, stand in the way of the clergy of the Church of England, when though very many and all *un*lawful they stood not in the way of Pope Alexander VI. and other pontiffs; besides instances of cardinals and priests in abundance? And why should not each clergyman be now, as in the apostles' days, " the husband of one wife, ruling well his own house, having his children in subjection?"—1 Tim. iii. 2, 4.

But these are all so many striking evidences of the deep-laid conspiracy against our Church; and, surely, men who thus deeply planned our ruin, would long since have accomplished their set purpose, were it not that a higher Power and a mightier hand is over us, preserving us in all our ways. So absurd was the proposal, so impossible the scheme, that even Mr. Oakeley is now obliged to acknowledge that

" it was castle building on a gigantic scale." And so indeed it was!

We need not follow Mr. Oakeley through the concluding portion of his lecture. It is made up of loose extracts from an anonymous work, of which Dr. Newman *now* admits the authorship, entitled, " Loss and Gain." We are the less careful to occupy these pages with matters of the kind, more especially as, according to Mr. Oakeley, Dr. Newman tells us, and truly, " that his tale is not founded on fact."

We have been so far dealing with actual facts; and are, therefore, not inclined to occupy time and space by dealing with acknowledged *fictions*. Fictitious tales can be brought to the defence of any system, and are not always the best mode of conveying instruction. Besides, in a matter of theological import, and in questions involving the vast and momentous differences between the Church of England and the Church of Rome, we cannot stay to listen to the morbid sentimentalities of imaginary young ladies of whom Dr. Newman has but little to say, and even admits that they " did not know themselves." Nor have we time in this serious controversy to hear out to the end the street gossip of an Oxford life, at least such specimens as are given in the lecture on the " Oxford Movement;" nor yet can we stay in our course to ponder the *dénouement* of a courtship—how Mr. W. and Miss B., instead of becoming, the one a monk and the other a nun, reappear in the far more pleasing relationship of husband and wife, and both still Protestants. Nor can we be expected to be possessed of patience to see how matters will turn up,—how another Mr. W. becomes a Roman Catholic, and Miss C. B. " makes her exit from the scene, without even a hint as to her future history." Mr. Oakeley and Dr. Newman may have time to devote to such topics, but we have not. We have far more serious matters to suggest to these men, and before we have done we may perhaps recall them from their visionary wanderings in the regions of romance to subjects of deeper moment to themselves and others.

The majority of the leaders and followers of the so-called " Oxford Movement " stand now in a very different position. They have changed sides, and are now responsible for all Romish doctrine. And now we are the more free to call them to account for their past deeds and excesses. It is no longer a few prayers from the Roman Missal that occupy attention, nor yet such orthodox passages as remain of the ancient forms, anterior to the apostacy or falling away of the Church of Rome. But now they are chargeable with *all* that the Missal contains—*all* that the Breviary enjoins—*all* that Popery teaches. It is one thing to talk in Oxford of a pious prayer in the Roman Missal, but it is quite another thing to be bound hand and foot in Rome, by each and every word it contains. It is one thing to import a stock of Breviaries into the University, but these men have ere this discovered that it is quite another thing to be held responsible for the legends, the marvels, the absurdities of the book itself. And herein is their weakness manifested. Having no option but to embrace the whole creed of Rome, they find themselves shut up, by their own consent, in a fortress which is capable of at best but a weak defence. Defend it they cannot, and therefore they shut up their harbours and fold themselves within their own mantles, and are satisfied so long as no immediate desolation comes nigh their home, even though the final issue is secured to *us* by the promise of Him, who when He promises forgets not to make it good. It is almost pitiable (but that they deserve it) to see men, who have by their former conduct, as made known to us by their " Personal Reminiscences," been foremost in every device and design of their own hearts, now brought down to a state of comparative inactivity;—men, who have planned amongst us deep counsels for aggression, now unequal to conduct even a weak defence;—men, who " secured free importations of Missals and Breviaries into Oxford," unable to defend either the one book or the other;—minds, that once ran after grand schemes, and gave no end of trouble, now met and kept at bay by the very weakest of instruments;—men, who while as Tractarians they continued in our ranks, dared even bishops upon their thrones, now, as Romish priests, cannot command a handful of Irish Romanists without a formidable curse and imprecation.* Is there not a cause?

Yes! This is the season of their weakness, because they are now no longer secret, but open, foes. They have now declared themselves, have cast off disguise, and appear in their real character. Once they made, in the moment of our remissness, a secret assault upon our lines—in studied speech they spake the *patois* of their school—half English, half Roman—and for a time deceived our sentinels, leaped into our trenches, wrought a degree of havoc among our people, penetrated to our inmost parallels, yea, even into our council chambers. These men " freely imported " the already burning fuses of the enemy into our camp, and laid them

---

* Curse pronounced by Rev. F. Oakeley, as by himself admitted.—*Guardian*, March 8th and 15th, 1854.

beneath the very pillow of those who cherished them; and waited to see the fatal issue. They systematically sowed dissension among our forces, and imbued the minds of many with principles of disloyalty and disaffection; and their labour "yielded several hundreds" of deserters to the enemy. And at length, having done their work, or apprehensive of detection should they continue in the camp, they deliberately passed over to the opposite lines, and already have we seen them assemble their people to tell the tale of their own baseness, and to render a statement of their " Personal Reminiscences " of the camp in which they had for a season sojourned.

To each individual member of the " Oxford Movement " we would say—" Nomine mutato, de te (*non* fabula) narratur:" Thou art the man! But now these men are not half so dangerous; and when brought into close encounter, are weakness itself. And it is only a matter of experience, the deepest cunning is ever accompanied by the greatest cowardice;—the most formidable secret foe is always the least formidable as an open enemy. Moreover, the strife and conflict between truth and error in these lands for the past few years have not been without their fruit and due result. The religion of Rome is better known to-day in England than it has ever been known since the days of her rule and goverance in these lands. The trumpet has given no uncertain sound—our people therefore have girt their loins for the battle. Sympathy with Rome there should be none. Rome that burned our martyrs—Rome that sought the desolation of our land—Rome that cursed our Queen of former days—Rome, that Sardinia disendows—Rome, that Spain deems a yoke too heavy—Rome, that Tuscany upholds by the incarceration of the children of God—Rome, that as it were on yesterday, added her latest article, and none can tell when she shall add the last, to her developed and still developing creed. This Rome, what sympathy should she have? what sympathy does she deserve?

Protest or sympathy? One or other may be selected—but both cannot co-exist in the same breast. Romanists we would love; we would labour and pray for them if, peradventure, we could rescue them from error. Romanism, positive Romanism we can understand, and deal with it as such. But those who in name protest against, and yet in heart sympathize with, the Roman system, these we cannot understand—they merit the respect of neither—the rights of neutrals we cannot for a moment entertain. " He that gathereth not with me, scattereth abroad."